BASKETBALL DREAMS

CHRIS PAUL

ILLUSTRATED BY
COURTNEY LOVETT

ROARING BROOK PRESS

NEW YORK

Published by Roaring Brook Press

Roaring Brook Press is a division of Holtzbrinck Publishing Holdings Limited Partnership

120 Broadway, New York, NY 10271 • mackids.com

Our books may be purchased in bulk for promotional, educational, or business use.
Please contact your local bookseller or the Macmillan Corporate and Premium
Sales Department at (800) 221-7945 ext. 5442 or by email at
MacmillanSpecialMarkets@macmillan.com.

Library of Congress Cataloging-in-Publication Data is available.

First edition, 2023

The illustrations in this book were created digitally. The text was set in Cronos Pro.
The book was designed by Mina Chung, the production was managed by Susan Doran,
and the production editor was Jacqueline Hornberger.
Printed in China by Toppan Leefung Printing Ltd., Dongguan City, Guangdong Province

ISBN 978-1-250-81003-8 (hardcover)

1 3 5 7 9 10 8 6 4 2

For Papa Chilly

—C. P.

To all the little dreamers,
and to the heroes that inspire them

—C. L.

My granddad Papa Chilly had dreams that came true,
so maybe if I listen and watch him,
mine will too.

I have basketball dreams
when I run out my front door,

down the sidewalk,
dribbling

and making jump shots
in the early morning.

I get to the court before anybody else
and feel like I'm the only person awake in the whole world
—except, probably,

my Papa Chilly, who's up before the sun even rises

and always says

the early bird

gets the worm.

Now

I do too.

Later on, after shooting free throws, I spend the day
at Papa Chilly's service station.

I hand him a tool as he
slides under a pickup truck.

People in the neighborhood
stop in to say hello.

Papa Chilly works hard,

showing

by

doing,

the first African American to own a

service station around here.

I have basketball dreams,

but sometimes I hear:

"You're too short"

or

"The court isn't for little kids."

But I don't listen 'cause Papa Chilly said

I have to

show

by

doing.

Papa Chilly also says you have to be there for your teammates and help them when you can.

He knows all about lending a hand

when others need someone to have faith in them.

I have basketball dreams as I bounce the ball down the street,
making sure I look both ways.

And I always make sure to say,
"Excuse me, sir" to Mister Ulysses and

BOUNCE!

"Sorry, ma'am" to Miss Rachel
as I dodge and run around them,
dribbling the length of my block

four,
five,
six times,
then back home again.

Then it's a barbecue in the backyard, and I am surrounded by family, happy noises, and all my favorite foods.

My big brother makes me smile while everybody talks about everything and nothing.

Laughter fills the air as Papa Chilly eats p

his favorite, wearing his famous over

his hands covered in grease from hard w

I have basketball dreams on game night
when I'm faster than most and feel like the basketball court is

where
I
belong.

And the cheers from my family, watching . . .
there's nothing like it.

Papa Chilly is here too—

as busy as he is, he never misses a game.

He's clapping so loud that somehow he's the only person
I hear.

And Papa Chilly's hands, slick with oil
from a long day at the shop . . .
they are working hands,
hardworking hands,
never-stop-working hands.

When I sail through the air, I hear Papa Chilly's cheers,

and

I lay

the ball

in the hoop

with a grin.

And nothing feels as perfect 'cause with Papa Chilly and
the rest of my family beside me, my basketball dreams,
like Papa Chilly's dreams,
just
might
come true.

My GRANDFATHER NATHANIEL JONES, nicknamed Papa Chilly, was born and raised in Winston-Salem, North Carolina, and ran the first Black-owned car service station in the state. He knew everyone in town, and everyone knew him. So many people relied on him and the station. I remember plenty of times seeing him just hand people money from the cash register out of the kindness of his heart, whatever they needed. If anyone in our family needed a job, Papa Chilly would hire them the very next day. No matter what I do in my life and career, my grandfather's legacy in Winston-Salem will forever be greater than mine—that's just the kind of impact he had.

As large as his legend loomed, though, my grandfather was never overt with his teachings; it was never "do this" or "do that," but he knew that people were watching, and as a kid, I'd sit back and learn like everyone else. I know the importance of respecting others, recognizing the value of hard work, and being a supportive father because my grandfather modeled that for me day in and day out.

I live the things he taught me to this day and pass them down to my kids and any others that I am able to impress his values upon as best I can. Without me even knowing it, Papa taught me to strive to be a good example and to chase my basketball dreams.